Two Lions

By William Marshall

This book edition 2022

Two Lions
By William Marshall

First published in North America by Endeavour Productions Ca Ltd
2022

Copyright William Marshall 2022
The Author asserts the moral right to be identified as the author of this work

ISBN book 978-17779317-9-7
ISBN Electronic Book 978-17782361-0-5
ISBN Other digital 978-17782361-1-2

All rights reserved. No part of this publication may be reproduced, stored in a retrieval system or transmitted in any form or by any means, electronic, mechanical, photocopying, recording or otherwise without the prior permission of the Author.

Table of Contents

Foreword	vii
Chapter 1	1
Chapter 2	13
Chapter 3	19
Chapter 4	27
Chapter 5	47
Chapter 6	51

I dedicate this book to the People of Ukraine.

Foreword

In my first book I described how my Intuitive Psychic abilities manifested when I was a kid and how my understanding of it had taken a significant step up when I met my first Mentor Claire and later when I had taken a 12-week course through Hays House with World Renowned Psychic John Edward. Later I explained how my numerous readings in many countries have come together to form my hypothesis of whether we really are here as a family pod of spirit each time we choose to come back or do we return as individual spirits and if so, why? My hypothesis which appears to be supported by Quantum Physics was something which came to me while taking stock of all my experiences together with my own past life regression and how that might be the key to my understanding of how it all works, life, the universe and everything. The book culminated with a warning from spirit of which I included the full transcript.

In this book, I want to try to explain how over 2020-2022 I started to try to identify as many pieces of the jigsaw, taking time to measure, objectively study and evaluate each piece through prayer and meditation to understand if it was a solid piece of evidence or just pseudo-science junk to be let go of. Though many times during my personal spiritual journey, I must admit I sat at my desk often wondering just what exactly I was looking for, I decided I simply didn't know, but I put my faith in knowing that I would no doubt recognize it when I found it.

Now, I'm just a regular, normal, everyday guy, perhaps the only exception is that I don't have a TV and instead prefer to read and think. Like most people I've had my fair share of ups and downs together with moments of personal crisis as well as fleeting occasions of complete bliss and happiness. The only difference is I am an Intuitive Medium and I have an enquiring mind, and it would appear that I seem to have glimpsed a bigger picture which seems to be coming ever more noticeable and yet most people choose to ignore. I say that because the more I work on my hypothesis, I can see that its very much evident for all to see. Hiding in plain sight, dressed up as an inconvenient truth by those who wish to shift your focus away for their own ends?

Since writing my first book *'Layers of the Universe' by William Marshall*, which amazingly seems on average to have had a velocity of 12, meaning for every copy sold, on average 12 other people have borrowed it and read it themselves before passing it on to someone else, I received many emails asking for more information, people seem to want to know about my next step of spiritual development and understand how they can use it in their own lives.

I think probably now is a really important point for me to just explain that while writing about my experiences and making them public, it's not my intention to deceive or entrap anyone. Neither is it my intention to distort truth or bring about negative impacts on others. I am merely describing my own personal spiritual journey which at first appeared nothing more than coincidental moments which were unconnected until more of the jigsaw began to fall into place. Your spiritual journey might be quite different. And that's okay!

Chapter 1

Firstly, I want to share some more experiences I had with spirit during my life in the hope that they help other people put their similar encounters into context and support others who are interested in Intuitive Mediumship together with readers who are curious about their own understanding of this essence called life and death or as I like to call it, life & life again!

When I was sick as a kid, after returning home from 10 weeks in hospital and continuing to get over the pituitary operation which had developed into a rampant case of Meningitis, I remember one night when I was finally back at home in my own bed, I woke up and the burning headaches I had been suffering from had gone. I was feeling really peaceful and suddenly I became aware of movement in the corner of my bedroom. Where the bedroom wall usually was, I saw a small figure dancing in the darkness. As I watched, it got bigger or perhaps closer until I realised it was an Amazon rainforest Indian dancing round and round. His face painted with bright colours and in one hand he held what looked like a cross between a child's rattle and a small drum on a stick which, as he twisted it back and forth, was rhythmically hit by small beaters on each side. Oddly enough I realised I couldn't hear either the chanting nor the sound of the drum, but I watched him for what seemed like ages, mesmerised. Instinctively I knew he was dancing to heal me. He was bathed in a green light from above and appeared to be dancing in slow motion. After some time, the scene finished and I was looking at my bedroom wall again.

Many years later, during the regular readings I was giving clients in Ukraine in 2014 & 2015, together with my translator, Tatiana, sitting in the kitchen of my old Soviet style apartment, I learned that just because we may have been born speaking one language in this life, spirit can still give me clear, accurate, validating information through images, emotions, physical sensations, and sounds no matter whether I know their native languages or not.

For example, I might be shown an image of a hospital drip. If the bag has clear liquid inside, there is no illness. If the liquid is tinted yellow, there is a treatable illness. On one occasion, a lady's husband had died. She asked if there was anything more she could have done to help? I was immediately shown a drip bag with dark brown liquid in it.

The answer, *"No, there was nothing you could have done but he loves you and thanks you for all the support you gave him"*

Another time in Canada, I went into a General Practitioners office to register as a new patient. The reception desk was empty. The waiting room empty. I waited and waited. Then I had an idea. In my head, I called my Spirit Guide to come to me and I asked if there were any spirit present. A moment later, the spirit of a middle aged, blonde nurse moved into view and looked at me. I smiled and acknowledged her and asked if she might be kind enough to influence someone living to come out and help me. A minute later, a receptionist came in and I was able to register. I thanked the spirit and left. Later that afternoon, while sitting in the front room reading, I became aware of the same spirit standing at the far end of my living room. I acknowledged her and she gave me the name Sylvia. She explained she had died from Cancer and she wanted me to tell her family that she is okay and that she is with them often. Unfortunately, however, I was unable to gain further information from her and couldn't identify her family members, so I add her to my book here in the hope that someone will recognise her and want to connect further.

It's often like that, no matter the country or the spirit, no matter how they died, the message is usually often the same, *"I'm okay, don't worry & I love you"*.

It made me consider that these answers would only make sense if we, like the allegory of the cave (which we will talk about later), are experiencing life here accepting it as the only reality, but that there is another place out of range of our five senses which is the equivalent of the sunshine, green grass, flowers, butterflies etc and naturally, what would you want to convey to someone who connected with you if you didn't have a lot of time or energy to pass on a message?

"I'm okay, don't worry & I love you!" sounds like the most obvious and efficient message.

Perhaps the most sublime experience I ever had was in late 2015, during an eight-hour flight from UK to Alberta, Canada, I wondered what might happen if I meditated and opened my chakras and senses on the plane. To my surprise, I found myself surrounded by what I presumed were angels, but they didn't look like angels in human form with wings, these were strange little white beings with small arms but no legs and with the most unconditional look of love in their eyes I have ever experienced. They beckoned me to join them outside the plane. Holding my hands, I was taken on a heart pumping, exhilarating trip in a semi-circle out over the left wing, around behind the aircraft and back in through the right side of the fuselage. I'll never forget it. It was freezing cold. I could feel the sensation of wind on my face and I knew I had to keep holding their hands as they stretched out either side of me. I looked at them and asked if I would be able to get back on the plane and they were all just smiling at me! I wanted to enjoy the moment but was pooping my pants wondering what would happen next if I couldn't get back onboard the plane.

As it happened, I did get back onboard and in meditation, saw myself get back into my body, breathe deeply and wake up. I sat looking down at the beautiful wide icy wastes of Greenland far below feeling exhilarated. I turned my head to look at my fellow passengers beside me, the big guy was fast asleep snoring like a gold medal winner, the lady in the aisle seat next to him was busily smiling at the male air steward with his gelled hair and perfect smile. Apparently, no one else had noticed my spiritual shenanigans.

I decided that the next time I flew alone, I'd try the same meditation to see if I could repeat the experience more than once. As it happens, because of the Pandemic lockdowns, I haven't had the opportunity but it's on my spiritual to do list.

In the early 2000's, I had walked into the Land Registry building in downtown Fredericton, New Brunswick, Canada not particularly thinking about anything when I noticed that I was walking on a black and white checker board ceramic tiled floor, it was freezing cold in there and a second later, I became aware that I was walking down between lines of dead pigs hanging from metal hooks in the ceiling. As soon as I realised what I was seeing, the vision was gone, it lasted maybe 3 seconds. Then suddenly I was in the warm modern hallway on my way to the office. It piqued my interest enough that I did some research and wasn't surprised to discover that over 100 years before, that building had been a butcher's shop. I get all kinds of experiences like this. These brief portals which appear and disappear, hinting at something else going on, or perhaps a glitch? It's why it's really important to dedicate specific times to open up as an intuitive medium and to ground yourself and close down and to be hard with yourself about it. But even so, just occasionally, even when I am closed down, I 'see' stuff which really started me thinking about what exactly might be going on.

Another part of the jigsaw came to me when I was giving a reading for a lady in my kitchen in Kyiv, Ukraine, the reading began as normal and pictures were coming to my third eye and I was describing them, but then something new happened. I began to feel a swaying motion, a magnetic swaying motion, from side to side. I hadn't experienced this before. I couldn't receive images for that moment, but intuitively I understood a spirit was about to come through. I stood up and was drawn to look at the living room. In a moment the swaying feeling became a visible cloud of tiny birds flying in a swarm from one side of the room to the other, high up on the ceiling before, suddenly they all formed together to create the form of a man. I can't explain this but surmise, as in quantum theory, particles were coming together to create a form in this plane of existence before later releasing back to form the fabric of the universe? Or more likely perhaps, the molecular membrane which separates both plains of existence.

Over the years I have been blessed to observe all kinds of phenomena such as just before my wife and I left Ukraine at the end of 2019 having been presented with a warning, her late mother had come through and said, "It would be in your best interests to leave Ukraine as soon as possible", then she had shown us a golden crown followed by a black hand from the east and graves across Europe to the horizon.

At the time we had thought it would be a massive Russian invasion but it turned out to be the Pandemic. Anyway, while we were waiting for my wife's visas to come through, I remember worrying that there would be some delay and we wouldn't be able to leave when the time came. A few days before she got her Visa's, I woke up one night and saw something on the bedroom wall.

Turning over in bed I looked again and could clearly see an illuminated outline of a fish and some other small symbols, a pair of wavy lines and a triangle etc.

Ordinarily I would have tried to check the source of them, but the heavy curtains were closed, the door shut and the room pitch black, so I didn't have to find a perfectly rational explanation such as light spillage from somewhere. These symbols had appeared, simply in this case, they existed and now they were shining there on the wall. I didn't need to find an explanation, intuitively I already knew that I was being given a sign that all would be okay.

The fear-based thinking had been gripping me, but now I relaxed immediately. It reminded me of the Bible story about Daniel and then I remembered at the time wondering whether the famous author JRR Tolkien might have also witnessed a similar phenomenon during his lifetime and used it in his book *'The Hobbit'* as moon letters? Had I seen a way that Spirit or the Universe or God communicates and has done so through the centuries? I have no explanation; I just know that I felt at peace after this experience.

Incidentally, in a different situation, maybe if the curtains would have been open, the door open, I'd have probably woken my wife up, annoyed with me, as I hunted around restlessly searching the bedroom for the source so

I would know absolutely that what I was seeing was easily explained and therefore I'd be able to decide a value for it. But in this case, the message to me was clear.

"Do not be afraid, everything is going to be okay".

I thought back to the man in the orange sweater who had picked me up, whilst hitchhiking many years before. It was 1993 and I had spent the summer hitchhiking in UK without a care.

I discovered that if, before starting my journey, I imagined in my mind's eye where I would stand on the road and the cars stopping for me, invariably once I was on the road, I would be picked up quicker and be more likely to arrive at my destination on time than if I didn't spend time imagining the trip beforehand. But there was one evening, I still had 35 miles to go to get home, it was late in the day and rain was setting in.

I had walked a couple of miles already and it suddenly struck me that it would be dark in an hour. I had no lights to illuminate myself with and there was no pavement on the road. I realised if it got dark and I still hadn't been picked up, there was a pretty good chance I'd be hit by a car in the dark countryside. So somewhat naively, I thought at the time, I had asked God to help.

Twenty minutes later, a man drove passed in an old orange car, he was travelling in the opposite direction, but he stood out because to my surprise he smiled and waved as he drove past. I watched him and wondered who he was. I was sure I didn't recognise him. Then a couple of minutes later, the same car came up beside me and stopped.

Thankful, I got in and the man said a funny thing,

"Sorry about that, I missed you and had to turn around", I smiled thinking it was a bit odd.

Then we drove all the way back to my hometown where I asked him to drop me off outside a supermarket. *"Don't you want me to drive you home?"* he asked.

I thought was quite an odd phrase. *"No thank you, I need to buy some milk first"* I said and we exchanged pleasantries and I got out thanking him. I crossed the road and he was gone. It struck me as a bit odd, but I stored the experience away in my head. Not realising it at the time but this was one of the first parts of the jigsaw.

Then of course another piece of the jigsaw which I experienced early on and still do from time to time is what I call 'the borrowers. Have you experienced 'the borrowers? You know, when you are looking for something, a tape measure, the car keys, the ointment you thought you had placed in the bathroom cabinet but when you go to find it, it's not there, so you hunt all over the house and a few minutes later, you go back and find it in exactly the same place you had already checked? Is it a glitch in time space? Or are you being tested? Are the watchers giving you a hint? Is the population so big that the great consciousness can no longer keep all the material things in existence at the same time and so, occasionally you spot a glitch? Or is he just seeing if you are paying attention?

Further, I began to notice in about 2010 during a long drive in UK, that if I observed I had been driving on a stretch of road and hadn't seen any other cars for quite a while, within 5 minutes, all kinds of cars would suddenly appear. And in 2019 when the train was late arriving to London's

Euston station and I only had 15 minutes to get across the city to London's Victoria train Station by taxi and it was rush hour, I had naively asked St Christopher, the patron saint of travellers to help, and the taxi had sailed through, all junctions offered green lights and we drove like a knife through butter. Even the taxi driver had remarked, *"Someone is looking after you!"* as he dropped me off at Victoria train station in record time. As I caught my train to the airport, I had mused that perhaps the great stage manager above had held back all the film extra's which star in my life film, out of the way to help me. Surely not?

Then there was the time at Vinnytsa Railway station when my wife and I were leaving Ukraine to travel to Cyprus. I had been suffering a severe bout of sciatica for two days before we were travelling and I was quietly worried about dealing with the luggage. The Ukrainian inter city trains are leviathans which don't meet the level of the platform, instead there is a climb up ladder-like steps hanging on to handrails before you can get into the train. How was I going to get two heavy suitcases up onto the train with my sciatica making me wince? On the morning we travelled, I had doped myself up on painkillers and was still hobbling around, giving an involuntary shout out in pain as I got both into and out of the taxi.

We struggled up to the platform and as the train came into the station, I mentally prepared myself with adrenaline pumping thoughts to get the bags onto the train with a last do or die effort. I'd deal with the pain once the train was moving. At the last second, out of the crowd a random man stepped forward and picked up my wife's luggage case, then mine and lifted them on board without even asking us if we needed help.

Did the Universe understand I needed help and send a helper?

I sat on the train with a cup of tea and looked out the window at the grey sky and mused. What if we could manifest anything? That sometimes it can take years, but we could actually manifest anything?

For instance, after Albert Einstein had contemplated the existence of Black Holes in the early 20th century and Indian astrophysicist Subrahmanyam Chandrasekhar in the 1930's had figured out the theory of how they might work, it would be Prof Steven Hawkins and Roger Penrose who worked out the particle theory seventy plus years later before finally Black Holes were discovered actually existing. Was this manifesting? Were Black Holes spoken or thought into existence?

A case of, *"If I can imagine this, it can exist?"*

If that's the case, can just anyone manifest absolutely anything at all?

Chapter 2

Manifesting – Here is how you really do it!

It's becoming clear to me that our ability to imagine and give heart felt, genuine appreciation to the Universe, Great Architect, God, The Great Watchmaker as some call him, for something we truly desire more than anything else is the basis to make that wish materialise. I've tested the hypothesis and it works, and the finer the detail you can create in your heart's desire and mind's eye, the more likely the Universe will deliver the exact same, but here is the thing, whatever you desire to bring to yourself materially, you have to add a final *"Or better"*, just to give the Universe some wiggle room as Alyssa Wood says.

Here is an example: My wife and I relocated to Cyprus for 6 months in 2018. The apartment was quite nice but we didn't have a stick of furniture apart from a leather sofa and a double bed. In one of the rooms which I hoped to use as an office, I looked forlornly at the empty space and in my mind's eye, imagined how the room should look. I was going to have a writing desk and that would be positioned on the left so I'd be able to see through the doorway and down the corridor to the front room from where I would be sitting. There was going to be a chair to go behind the desk. Against the opposite wall I imagined a bookcase and in the far corner, I decided I would like a small comfy armchair. For about a month I kept imagining the room and how I would feel while I would be working in there. It was almost like; I was expecting the furniture to be there at some time in the future. Or actually, I believed that the furniture was already there at some point in the future and I'd just have to wait for the time to pass before I could see it. I gave my ever-patient wife a tour of the empty room describing where everything would go. I even mimed sitting in the chairs and getting books from the bookshelf. We had no money, the school I had interviewed for successfully, started delaying the start date and we were in the poop.

About two months later, we were walking past the Landlady's house and saw some furniture in the yard. She was reading a book outside. *"Moving out?"* I asked.

"No," she said, *"I've bought new furniture for my daughter's room and I am waiting for these to go to the junk yard. Do you want any of them?"*

I cast my eye over it...there was a cheap bookcase, an old well-worn leather armchair, a small writing desk and a swivel chair. I laughed. *"I'll take all of it!"*

So, inadvertently, I realised that I had in some way, attracted the stuff I needed for my office. But it didn't match and wasn't exactly as I had imagined. That's when

I realised that in order for the Universe to help, when you manifest, you have to be absolutely specific in what you ask for. Colour, age, quality, size, all and then add the main winning part *'or better'* so the Universe has some extra room to provide it.

This is what I do now when I want to manifest, *"I would like a brown leather arm chair without rips and that has come from a non-smoking, animal free home. I would like a tall brown bookcase with four shelves that are adjustable and made of wood, I would like a wooden office desk with draws on one side and an open space for my computer tower on the other, with a sliding keyboard shelf and a matching office chair, or better"*

By doing this, I experimented and discovered that at first, I got mixed results and got better results when I added *'or better'* at the end. I also have noticed a time difference too between manifesting small stuff and bigger stuff. Currently I'm manifesting my first house with a garden and two car garage in a specific part of the world, it's been two years so far and is going to take a little longer, but eventually I believe it will be made available for us. However, the manifesting is only half of the equation, having patience and faith in the universe are huge factors too. How many of us ask the Universe for something and then give up after 3 months because it hasn't happened yet?

While the universe wants us to sit in our canoe, let go of the paddle and allow the river to take us to our destination with peace, happiness and faith that every opportunity we need will be offered to us from the riverbanks as we travel, instead, what do we all do? We find ourselves picking up the paddle, aiming at some point at the top of the waterfall behind us and paddling crazily backwards against the current with passion and desire to get us up above the waterfall to where we are sure we want to be.

Not surprisingly most fail and then feel dejected because nothing has worked out for them. Remember, the universe can't give you money necessarily, but it will give you opportunities which can result in more money flowing to you. However of course, money isn't everything, perhaps people want other things to come to them, however, the process is the same.

It suddenly occurred to me that the best thing you can do, if you want to manifest, is first choose what would make you happy, start doing it and just by relaxing, going with the flow and continuing to do it, the opportunities come to meet people, go places, show your work, become recognised and receive more opportunities and so on. We don't need the heartache, the anxious fighting against the current to reach our goals, we need to have the courage to find something we like to do and follow the river.

However, before I could do that, I decided I should step through the old habits to see a new side of me and ask myself why do I feel this way? Asking and answering this question was directly tied to my values as a person and I decided it would lead me to a lot of truth and I'd need that before bringing the jigsaw together.

Perhaps the last and in some way most vital part of successful manifesting is to let go of the over analyzing, calculating numbers and making detailed time lines. The overanalyzing kills it. Just let the universe deliver it in a way that makes sense to it and be ready for some wonderful surprises.

Chapter 3

Emotion code stuff

Maybe it was because after my first divorce I had been living the life of a nomad for 10 years, rattling around all over the world, living here and there, teaching English and never really having any personal items. It was a long time before I found the inner peace I was looking for. In fact, once I began to settle and take stock, I realised that I would have described my mental outlook at that time as follows, I was a lone soldier, in enemy territory, carrying a heavy rucksack on my back, travelling at night, trying to find friendly lines. It was utterly exhausting living that way and living in such a *'fight or flight'* state was the worst for my Addison's disease too.

This realisation made me appreciate it was time to let the emotional baggage go, but I had no idea how to do that, I had just been mentally cutting around anything resembling a painful memory until finally in April 2020, having found a townhouse to rent and settle into, I started to put down roots and naturally began to decompress past events from my life.

Or maybe it was the global lockdowns during the Pandemic which made me go a little bonkers, I'm not absolutely certain. But after two years of somewhat enforced reflection, I believe I, like many people at that time, began to find themselves evaluating their lives up to that point.

"*What were the good things I'd been involved with? What things could I be proud of? and What things might I have done differently or better if I had a second chance?*" I wondered quietly.

I would be washing up or having a cup of tea, looking out the window, or else falling asleep last thing at night and realised I was quite without planning it, beginning to decompress the last 20 years +

Though my wife was kind enough not to point a finger at me and mention it, I began to be aware that I was becoming more emotional.

I realised perhaps it was time for me to delve deeply into my past life and explore all the hurt, resentment, hate, anger, feelings of injustice and examine any and all bad decisions I had made. During the process, I sat quietly, meditating and these explorations inside myself sometimes lasted 20 minutes and other times all night. I even woke up on the floor in the spare bedroom one morning after not realising my meditation had become dreams and I had evidently slowly crumpled onto the carpet, only to wake up when the sun began to shine on my face the next morning. To my surprise, I found it a positive experience and felt lighter and more relaxed.

Initially in the first meditations, I found myself dealing

with recent events which in some cases were fresh in my mind and in others I discovered things which had been triggered by occasions that hadn't even registered as such on my conscious mind at the time they happened.

Whenever I found myself drawn to hurtful words from childhood, or frustrating situations, or events which had really deeply affected me, I spent time to analyse what had happened, how I might have dealt with them better and then I began to replay them in my mind's eye with different potential outcomes. Over time, I found I was able to go through some past situations a hundred times and if they had originally been negative and hurtful, I was able to imagine what the outcome could have been if something positive had happened instead and, in this way, I managed to put to bed a lot of hang-ups which I hadn't realised had had such a negative effect on me. I was also able to relive some memories that consciously I had been labelling as traumatic events, only to find that in introspection, they appeared to have absolutely no hold over me at all.

Eventually I was able to get right back to childhood events and not only relive them, reprocess them and let them go, but I was also able to see my adult self, visiting my childhood self in my bedroom when I was a kid and sitting on the edge of the bed and telling my little self that everything was going to be okay, I was a good lad and I was proud of him and all he would do in future.

In time, I also realised that there were elements of my teenage years, for example when my parents divorced which I had held onto well into adulthood and which were not doing me any favours. I decided it was time to send the big fat emotional wobbly teenage part of myself away. But how? Was it possible to partition my emotions?

Over a few weeks, the answer came to me. I did a meditation asking to be shown a house where my emotional teenage self would be happy to live. It was no surprise that with my love of Celtic history, I was shown an ancient Celtic circular mud hut with a thatched straw roof. So, over a number of months, I would venture to the roundhouse during meditations and in my mind's eye, I started to build dividing walls, taking great satisfaction in weaving the willow among the upright staves to create wattle panels.

Then I created a central hearth. Next came the clay beehive shaped oven. Then an upper floor where I could store supplies for myself. Evening by evening, week by week, I would meditate and go to the Mud hut and add some little detail. I built a clay kiln and fashioned pots, jugs, bowls and such, fired them and then stacked them for use. I made clay amphoras and filled them with red wine. I stuffed a linen mattress with horse hair and linen pillows with dried springy sphagnum moss.

It was a journey of the heart. The satisfaction I felt was immense and gave me peace in my conscious everyday life. Interestingly, after filling the house with decoration including beeswax candles, oil lamps and food, I went to the Roundhouse one night only to discover an older grandmother figure standing baking small buns in the clay oven. This took me by surprise.

Until that moment, I completely believed that what I was creating in my mind's eye was only for myself. So, the discovery that other entities can turn up there shocked me. Was the woman a spirit joining me to be there to support my fat wobbly emotional teenage self? Or had my subconscious created her? I had no idea. However, towards the end of the meditations, I found myself moving in, lighting the fire, drinking wine and feeling completely at peace there. So, it didn't surprise me at all when one evening, I walked into the mud hut only to find an acquaintance from my historical re-enactment days, who had died many years ago, sitting by the fire dressed in ancient Celtic costume.

I welcomed him. But until that moment hadn't even imagined that my meditated creation might attract other spirits? *"So, the place I created in my mind's eye was like a cloud, accessible to others in spirit?"*

In meditations, I looked to Epona the white pony from the ancient Celtic stories to come and take me there. It was a place I could be free to ride horses, and stop being so British and apologetic about everything. I filled the roundhouse with baskets of gear, amphorae of red wine and even some cigars. I took pride collecting the small kindling and then cutting bigger kindling and then logs. Lighting the first fire in the round house and then on subsequent nights, I built charcoal clamps out in the woods to create fuel for the fire.

Then I took a draw knife and formed wooden lids with little knob handles for the clay jars. Sheep skins lay all around and I stitched a horse hair mattress and carved a wooden chair for myself to sit in by the fire. Even so, I always preferred to lie on the sheepskins next to the fire. All the cares of the world left me until one evening I realised during my Shadow work, that it was time for me to send my fat emotional teenage self, there for good. On the evening of the meditation, as I planned to send that part of my personality away on Epona, I whispered in the pony's ear, *"Don't bring him back"*.

The next day when I woke up, I realised I felt different. Better, calmer, more able to cope with everything. I had a greater level of inner peace and that continued.

The inner peace was a welcomed break from the noticeably strange reception returning to settle in Canada had given me. At the same time as being on my spiritual journey, I had found myself almost constantly being ignored by all the Government agencies, Medical Agency, Banks, Lawyers, despite all my attempts to make connections to register for services or ask for help as a newcomer to Canada, frustratingly all the websites kept giving me repeated error signs, or when I called them, the auto voice directories would just hang up.

In a fit of frustration, I wrote physical letters and sent them recorded delivery to head offices and again, never received answers. I was feeling pretty much unwelcomed and couldn't understand what I was doing wrong to receive such stonewalling? Little could I imagine that by the Spring of 2022, all would begin to make sense.

A few weeks later, I ventured back to the roundhouse during a meditation and had a little look inside. My fat emotional wobbly kid self, had lost no time at all and was smoking cigars, drinking red wine and had been joined by a whole tribe of people, all listening to live folk rock music, dancing and drinking and having a great time.

Three months later, I was standing in the kitchen making dinner with my wife when I suddenly was presented with a mental picture of my fat, emotionally, wobbly self, smiling and waving, riding Epona back towards me. I thought about it and felt a tiny feeling of dread for a second before communicating with the pony.

I said, *"No way! Don't bring him back!"*

But here is the thing, by the end of the year, I found myself feeling once again, too emotional. Maybe it was because I had quit smoking after 35 years and my body chemistry was all over the place? I was unsure. If I had had to describe how I was feeling, I would have described it as, I was a little boy in a dark cave. In the cave was a dragon. I knew that if he saw me, if I made a sound, or moved, he'd see me and eat me. So I had to stand against the wall in the darkness hoping he wouldn't open an eye and find me. Then, during meditation it came to me. Remember I had created this alternative place and tended it and added to it and visited it regularly, whilst I was doing that, I was giving it life and some would say, I was starting to exist in two separate realities. It suddenly occurred to me that, for 6 months I had not been tending to it neither had I been visiting it. I decided to call the horse and have her take me back to the roundhouse. To my surprise, the house was empty, deserted, bare inside. I rationalized that I had created this partition in my brain to isolate the overly emotional self, but that in time it had faded away.

I read a book about Psychology and discovered that by creating alternative realties in my mind and feeding them to the point whereby my waking reality wasn't the main avenue of my life, I was actually quite close to giving myself a mental illness.

Chapter 4

Shadow work

About a year later, it occurred to me that perhaps I could use the same technique to attract what I would like for the future? Perhaps figuratively rather than physically. So, after careful consideration, I chose Victorian England. During mediation, I would spend my nights in Victorian England, sitting next to a fireplace above which hung a large mirror, the wooden floor covered mostly in the centre by a heavily patterned rug. With wooden writing desk, newspapers from between 1875 and 1914 to read. I sat and read in my high-backed chair, in my Victorian trousers, brogues, white shirt and tie with waistcoat and occasionally smoke some pipe tobacco and listened to the gentle ticking of the clock, before I fell asleep and woke up here as normal.

In Victorian England I was older, wiser, more at peace and able to think clearly. I would read about something in the old newspaper and discuss it out loud with occasional spirit visitors who appeared there from time to time. Then

I began to create the rest of the house and later still, I began to create the garden where I would plant vegetables after they had come out of the greenhouses. Then I built the barn which would house the alpacas and saw myself getting up at 5am shaking feed buckets for them. Perhaps the Bible is true, what we create in this world, we find in the next world? I really hadn't formed an answer to that until other spirit had begun to inhabit what I created without me actually intending it to happen.

Then the thought struck me, *"What if I go to Victorian England one night and don't come back?"*

By my big October 2021 monthly meditation, freaky stuff started happening. I read about the theory that everything is energy vibrating at different speeds and that really began messing my brain up. I remember walking up the street imagining everything, houses, trees, grass, cars, lampposts all vibrating and telling myself its all an illusion and that both quantum physics and information from spirit guides was telling me that none of these things were real. They were only there because I needed them to be there to give context to my current existence.

Then one afternoon, after entering meditation I felt I had hit the motherlode. The information began to come forward showing me a cartoon version of the Lion wearing a crown. Then I began to see all weird shapes and colours. A stone cross against a purple sky, then I saw more weird flowing almost Kaleidoscopic patterns of day-glow colours, a flowing river which became a sea on a shoreline at night. Finally, I saw five thin silver figures sitting on what appeared to be flying or hovering silver legless seats in a red and black room with what appeared to have the outline of a five-pointed star etched onto the floor beneath them.

"What is this? What am I seeing?" I asked my Spirit guide.

"It's another dimension" he answered

"But it's all gobbledegook?" I answered

"The longer you spend in it, the more it will make sense" he said.

"Who are these silver figures?" I asked

"They are you!" came the answer.

Perplexed, I closed down completely. Something obviously wasn't right, maybe I had tried too hard and finally was attracting gibberish energy and pictures?

About a week later, I was waking up one morning and I saw the lion beside my bed. Intuitively I was given the following message: *"You might inadvertently trigger a mental illness. Stop Now."*

This had a sobering effect on me and I closed right down, stopped giving readings and stopped meditating for 6 months. I felt like I was in free fall. What did all this mean? Further, not only was I continuing to receive gibberish signs in meditation, I found myself having terrible times in shops and restaurants. Waitresses didn't serve my wife and I for ages, even though we had been sitting at the table waiting the catch the waitresses' eye. In shops, I'd be waiting patiently to pay and the sales clerk would ignore me and serve other people. It seemed that in Alberta, only when you started shouting and waving your arms about using words like, *"Baffled!"* and *"Incompetent"* did the shop staff actually tune into our presence. I couldn't fathom it at all. It was like we were invisible.

I had the realisation maybe it could be a Vitamin B3 deficiency causing hallucinations & visions when one evening a couple of months later, I decided to open myself up again in meditation one last time and was surprised to see all my relatives who are in spirit had turned up. However, none of them were smiling. It was odd, usually they were all standing in the light and smiling, sending me positive nice thoughts. This time they were all standing back in a semi-circle of darkness looking at me as if they were concerned. None of them spoke.

I remember I was kneeling down wondering why they weren't giving me mental pictures as usual when suddenly a freaky looking, glowing woman with mesmerising eyes walked into the dark room. She was kind of a caricature of an old woman with grey hair in a double bun, wearing an odd top hat and a tartan blanket for a long skirt. It partly made me want to laugh as I immediately labelled it, *"The little old Welsh woman from hell"* as it appeared to echo the traditional costume of Welsh women in my home country. But it was hypnotising, the more this glowing entity looked at me, I felt an overwhelming pull to accept it into my life, I wanted to like it and follow it, I wanted to know more, I felt a desire for it to become part of me. Then, I looked past it at my silent relatives and realised I had to cut the connection.

I don't know what it was. It wasn't spirit. The freaky glowing old woman smiled at me and took a step closer and I thought,

"No freaking way!".

I closed down immediately. Grounded myself. Put the lights on, went downstairs, poured a big glass of wine for myself and hunted for the ancient packet of cigarettes I hid years ago *"for emergencies"*. I can handle most things but that mesmerising glowing woman put the screaming heebie jeebies up me.

I lay in bed the next morning after an uneasy night sleeping with the lamp on hoping I wouldn't suddenly wake up and see the creepy glowing Grandma in top hat smiling at me from the corner of the room.

This was the beginning of a really tense time. I had started my YouTube channel '*William Marshall – Intuitive Medium*' in an effort to meet people from all over the world, or different faiths and nationalities to discuss faith, spiritualism, religion, atheism to try to help me understand the big picture. But soon after making 10 or so episodes, I noticed that I was starting to receive psychic attacks and they were starting to have a noticeable unpleasant effect on my life. During the day, I noticed that most were coming through astral projection. I had even *'seen'* the grey coloured entity coming up the stairs as I sat reading on the sofa. I closed the book and fired white light at the entity. The grey figure didn't like that and left howling.

I sat quietly and looked out the window one afternoon. It occurred to me that none of this was normal and I might be falling down, emotionally, mentally and physically. Obviously, I was having some kind of mental health breakdown? Was it the two years of almost complete isolation in the apartment during the Pandemic which was the cause? Or had I asked to be shown the secrets of the universe only to receive a massive brain collapse trying to understand the reality of it all?

Other times it would present as an argument between my wife and I for no connected or apparent reason, from out of nowhere. We stood looking at each other with mildly puzzled looks on our faces and almost together asked each other out loud, *"Where did that come from?"*

It would have been unusual because we had never had a bad word between us, except that we had experienced similar when we lived on Cyprus.

Back in 2018 whilst walking between the castle and the immigration office on Larnaka's beachfront, my wife and I had experienced a sudden argument out of nowhere as we walked beside the beautiful clear sea, under the shining gorgeous sun in lovely warm temperatures. It was so odd, we noticed it as something unusual but decided to let it go and think nothing of it. Two weeks later, when we walked back the same way, guess what, we had another argument, out of the blue in exactly the same part of the seafront. Whatever energy is hanging around Larnaka beachfront is one thing, now something similar was coming into our house on the other side of the world and messing with us!

In early 2021, over a week or two, we became aware there was also something else coming into the house and affecting us. Almost imperceptible at first, out of the blue, we would both suddenly get the thought that we should prepare and pack our most treasured possessions in grab bags because the house was going to burn down while we were asleep. I would receive this thought process while I was upstairs only to discover that my wife had experienced exactly the same thought process downstairs in the kitchen.

Other times, we were aware that we were being observed in our otherwise empty living room. This was characterised by a strange mildly sickly magnetic feeling in an otherwise empty room. Occasionally, my wife would uncharacteristically have terrible nightmares and sometimes I received intuitive messages which sounded like a toxic person taking the piss out of something I was doing.

This happened on three separate occasions. Sometimes, when I had caught it by the neck, waiting for angels to come so I could give it to them to deal with, I observed that the life-sized grey entity had no face, other times it had what appeared to be a steel plate across where its eyes should be and all I could feel was misery and lack of hope emanating from it.

Intrigued, I began writing down when and where things were observed, times events were happening and described them in a notebook. Over time it became evident that, there were two things occurring. The astral projected attacks were happening at a time corresponding with a man I knew from UK. I was shown that he was behind some of the attacks. Some of the other stuff was connected to each time we went to a small super market near the house. I surmised that every time we went to the shop, a parasitic entity or spirit was latching onto us and following us home.

This was borne out when during a meditation, I saw him. A young man with long wavy dark hair and bright mischievous dark eyes laughing at me from the corner of the room. He was wearing older style clothes, from the 80's maybe. He thought he was invincible until I used the nuclear warhead of spiritual warfare against him. I actually felt the sensation as he was catapulted clean out of the house and out across to another part of the city on Archangel Michael's sword. I felt the sensation of him landing on the asphalt of a parking lot a few miles away and I also felt the shock he felt from being given the good news, probably for the first time ever. After that we didn't experience anything again for a few months until we picked up another different parasitic entity from, oddly enough, the same shop.

Overall, the experiences made us think. My wife isn't psychic and yet she was being affected by outside elements on another plain of existence. If it could happen to us who are aware, how much of the same experiences are happening to other regular people all over the world who are unaware? And how many lives have been changed, either at work or in relationships where both parties consider that one or both acted 'out of character' or wonder why they had even argued in the first place? It got to the point that we were experiencing the psychic attacks so much, that in the end finally, I sat down and started to read as much as I could about psychic phenomena in an effort to find out more.

By June the Psychic attacks were becoming almost incessant. It felt like we were constantly both under hammer blows being rained down on us. One morning, after another sleepless night, I didn't meditate, I actually found a quite spot in the house, knelt down and prayed for the first time in years and chose to ask to have myself and my family sealed within the blood of Jesus Christ.

To my surprise, almost instantly, the psychic attacks stopped as if a light switch had been thrown. My wife noticed it was a much lighter atmosphere in the house too.

Over the next two days, I found myself in quiet contemplation, trying to accept, rationally as many of the parts of the jigsaw I had already discovered even if not all the present pieces fit each other.

I sat with a cup of tea and pondered to myself. If, by committing to being sealed in the blood of Jesus, all the psychic phenomena had ended, then it couldn't have been a mental illness episode that I had been suffering from? Could it? No medication was administered. The phenomena had just been silenced by an intense personal spiritual choice.

Clearly, it was time for me to stop for my own good.

However instead, I decided to completely throw myself into all the shadow work and in-depth psychic work that I could. I met new spirit guides, one of which, let's call him 'G' appears only as an outline with what appears to be a wobbly flower on his forehead which moves as he speaks. I was told I am far older than I can ever imagine, this made me wonder whether if reincarnation is true then perhaps, I am just a very slow learner because I keep getting sent back!

"G" also told me that there is so much more about

existence that I can never know all of it. That I have existed and exist now in many different dimensions at the same time.

"*More quantum physics!*" I thought.

However, it was after that, that things really started happening full on psychically to me and even my family. And not only psychically, things were beginning to hint of religious experiences and surely to me that wasn't necessarily a sign of positive mental health? I felt I had to be careful.

One afternoon, my wife and I were meditating together and a massive golden orange serpent appeared. Not only was it the size of a python, I felt it physically crawling up my left arm, around my shoulders and then it whispered in my right ear starting with the words, *"Mark my words..."*

Later, after making a cup of tea, I researched this golden serpent on line and a website declared that if I see the Golden serpent than I have really made it to a high level of consciousness that few ever reach. But after weighing up the evidence, I took this with a pinch of salt because I later read in another site, the devil is described as a Python.

This encounter was the first time I became conscious of the Bible. Sure, I'd tried to read it loads of times before, but every time I seemed to either have a brain crash trying to understand the style of writing used or it seemed to me you could interpret anything you read in it in any number of different ways. I always put it down feeling a bit confused and really none the wiser. So, I decided that if there is a God, and if he wanted me to believe in him, then I offered to be a vessel for him, through which he would do amazing God-like things. I meant it quite reverently and really willingly decided to place myself in that position to see what might occur, if anything.

A few days later, in a meditation, I suddenly had the sensation of falling down through the floor and observed I was hanging over what looked like the inside of a volcano, with a lake of fire at the bottom. As I looked, I began to see, in the lava, covered forms of screaming figures in the magma. The heat was intense. Then I became aware that I was being held by one arm above me. Held by whom? I had no idea.

Not sure what to do, Instinctively, I projected a shield of white light downward like a large upside-down umbrella below me and filled the neck of the volcano with it. I was unsure what to do next but, in a moment, a golden light appeared above me, and through the shield I was projecting, thousands and thousands of souls started rising up through the shield and into the light. It went on for minutes and was mesmerising. I realised immediately that I was indeed being used as a vessel by the higher power.

That afternoon, I went downstairs, made a coffee with a spoonful of whisky in it and had a good think about what I had just experienced. It quickly became apparent; I'd started something in motion and it would appear God liked me.

The next day, during a meditation, to my astonishment, a lioness came through the wall, looked at me, lay down in front of me and then visited repeatedly during the next three meditations. I googled it. The lioness is the hunter. I thought about that for a while and decided maybe she was out searching for believers?

Some weeks later a different, this time weird looking lion appeared. He had a dark mane and blue freaky eyes, I felt uneasy sitting with him standing before me. He kept appearing. Never made a noise, neither did he impart any kind of obvious knowledge intuitively. But I always felt unsettled in this lion's presence. I had no idea what was going on, but these were all parts of my jigsaw and I just collected them and decided everything would fit into place eventually.

Then, within a month, the weird dark maned mangy looking lion appeared in front of me again, but then to my surprise suddenly another, bigger golden lion appeared behind me. There was an immense feeling of calm and peace from the new blonde lion. He walked forward, roared silently and the dark maned lion turned and walked away through the wall. I had absolutely no idea what was going on. I just observed and tried to draw conclusions over the long-term. And why could I never hear the sound? I still have absolutely no idea.

From that time onward, the big blonde lion has visited often. Now he appears even when I am not in meditation. Now, do I believe I am really seeing a lion? Of course not, I can only accept that spirit is coming to me in a form that I can accept.

Thinking back to my childhood it is no surprise because I loved the C.S Lewis Narnia adventures which feature Aslan the lion. So, symbolically, this answered why a lion should appear to me. Perhaps for someone else on their spiritual path the God entity would appear in a totally different form but one which that person could accept too.

First the large blonde lion appeared and he told me, *"Get fit!"*

Then a week later he appeared and rather cryptically said, *"I need obedient soldiers"*

Then some days later he appeared and said in a more ominous tone, *"Why aren't you getting fit? If you knew what was coming, you would be getting fit now!"*.

In another monthly meditation, he said *"There is something not particularly nice in this house with you. Only listen to the messages of love".*

I went for a long walk to get fit and thought about all this.

"You'd be getting fit if you knew what was coming" repeated in my mind and still often does. What am I being warned about?

Is there some great catastrophe coming? Meteorite impact? Nuclear Warhead detonated off the coast of California that would lead to a Tsunami and Catastrophic Subduction? Or is this all a test to see if I accept fear-based thinking over love-based thinking?

This experience made me consider the 10 years when I had lived and worked in Ukraine, almost imperceptibly, I had always felt that there might have been a need to leave quickly. Now, with the 2022 Invasion of Ukraine by Russia having become a terrible reality, I began to wonder if, as I had picked up this vibe of invasion many years before, I wondered if people who call themselves *'Preppers'* around the world had also tuned into some other vibe which has been resonating on a plain of existence for many years and is building? Almost an imperceptible call to prepare?

But then I wondered why would this be so? if God was planning to end our existence finally, would he not allow the larger section of society to feel this almost intuitive, imperceptible portent? But then I read that perhaps the faithless are purposely having such things hidden from them.

I thought back to the time I was visiting Maine, USA in 2003, I just happened to meet a guy I had briefly served with in the army in 1990 before I was scrubbed and medically discharged for not informing them about my Addison's disease. I had enjoyed nine glorious months, in my element, having the time of my life, which I felt for years wasn't supposed to end, and felt bitterly about losing, until during my shadow work, whilst inspecting those feelings, it was suddenly revealed to me,

"Not this time William, the army is not for you in this life you have to follow a different path"

When I met him, I was surprised to discover that whilst I had been travelling around the world without a care, teaching English and exploring life, he on the other hand had been preparing for the end of the world. He had built a house on a hill with a 360 field of view and in his basement, and attic for that mind, he had more rifles and ammunition to hand than an average army battle group might carry.

As we sat sipping the NATO standard tea, black tea with one sugar, in his front room, I just happened to notice the 9mm pistol on top of his bookcase and the baseball bat, glove and ball leaning against the corner of the room beside the door. In the kitchen apart from extra sets of firing pins I discovered in his cutlery draw, while hunting for a teaspoon, I noticed the plethora of Gurkha Kukri's, Japanese Samurai swords and Zulu shield and spear bedecking his walls, not to mention fire extinguishers in strategic places and the 10 years of preserved food and fresh water he had tucked away.

I couldn't help thinking that if a Police officer inadvertently knocked the door to innocently enquire on a neighbour one evening, then my friend would probably be instantly triggered, blow his house up and enjoy his very own "*Azovstal last stand*" from the rubble, keeping whoever, '*they*' might be at bay for three months before they finally got him.

I sat on the sofa in his living room and sipped my tea as a war film thundered away on the television. Errol Flynn was single-handedly liberating Burma from the Japs in Black and White. I finally plucked up the courage and asked my friend what had got him into prepping and what he was expecting?

He answered with a sober, straight face, *"The screaming hordes of Chinese mon ami!, I give it five years and they'll be screaming 100 abreast and a 1000 deep down the street and I'll be giving them the good news, they'll wish they'd never invaded"*

I gazed at the TV nonchalantly nodding trying to see things from his point of view, then he added,

"*Besides, knowing I'm prepared, I sleep better. I don't worry about anything anymore; I've got it covered*".

I didn't know what to say, so I smiled and said, *"Nice one mate!"*

As I backed the car out of his drive and waved *"Au revior!"*, I cut around it mentally and went about my regular day. But I never forgot him. Now, 20 years later, I realise it's all relevant to what I am discovering and learning about now. The fear-based thinking versus Love-based thinking. There is a subtle pattern and its repeating.

This was an important connection of two or more jigsaw pieces for me because for weeks after seeing the big blonde lion appear and I had asked him what I should be preparing for. I began receiving mental films in my head during meditations which I couldn't control. They were automatically playing as if I was watching a movie quality version of a First-Person Shooter Video Game and actually had the effect of my heart racing, blood pressure up as if I was actually there taking part in what they showed me. Most began with me living in a nice house in the countryside, I would get a phone call from an old local man warning that three quarry trucks full of looters or trouble makers were on their way up to plunder & burn my house down.

I was shown again and again, me shooting and scooting, sometimes in the darkness and other times in daylight using Molotov cocktails to hit them in the backs of the lorries before they could organise, then sniping at them from both outside and inside my house. My heart would be booming in my chest as I *'saw'* these movies in my head. Sometimes the *'film'* would see just myself fighting alone and other times there would be five or six helpers with me.

But oddly, every time, though scenarios changed, I began to realise that each time I was *'shown'* this dramatic film, I always won. So, still unsure what it was, I decided it must just be symbolic but of what I couldn't tell. Was I being warned of a future event? Or was it an astral projected demonic attack culminating in the most terrifying scare tactics he could impress upon me? Or was it simply a way to show that I am stronger than I realise and can overcome even the worst situations? Or was this the example of the negative energy living in this house with us whom we had been warned we should ignore and only accept the love-based information instead? I couldn't be absolutely sure.

Then one afternoon the lion gave me another ominous warning,

"The earth will shrug"

and about a week later I stumbled upon a lecture in YouTube about geology called 'Catastrophic Subduction' by Dr Kurt Wise, I suggest you make a cup of tea one afternoon and watch that.

Then by November's monthly meditation, I suddenly found myself sitting on a mountainside, surrounded by a sea of beautiful flowers. The lion sat beside me on my left. From here, I could see in the distance a wide river encircling around us. Then across the river, I saw every part of the earth, like it was spread out on one flat plain before us. European farms, deserts with the spires of mosques, freezing white antarctica in the far distance, Rocky Mountains and steaming jungles. It was a beautiful view. You could see everything from there. It gave me great inner peace. I wanted to sit there forever.

That afternoon, I prepared to go to bed at 4pm, so I could wake up at 2am to begin teaching English to students from across the other side of the world. They were tough days and the lack of sleep probably wasn't helping my overall mental outlook. Before I went to bed, I sat and told my wife what I had just experienced above. I explained we were being asked to be prepared to look after people in the future when they needed us.

We read through all of the information which had been shared with me and then I went to sleep on it. No other psychic's I knew had ever mentioned such information coming through for them. I doubted its veracity, the chaotic doomsday information seemed too incredible to be taken seriously. I left the notebook with all my notes I had written down during my meditations with my wife and went up the wooden stairs to bed.

In bed, just before I fell asleep, I thought back to the first time I had found myself on the hillside beside the lion during another meditation in 2008, I had sat and cried and complained and moaned about just how crap my life was and how nothing was working and how everything I tried failed and was just about to continue with my *'woe is me'* self-pity when I realised the Lion was ignoring me. Well, at least he wasn't pandering to me or even trying to calm me with placation.

He was sitting watching the world silently, calmly, peacefully, patiently in control. It struck me just how long suffering he is. He gives someone the physics to create free, clean nuclear energy for all and the first thing we do is create a bomb to kill millions with it. I decided to stop feeling sorry for myself, apologised and before I left, I am sure I saw the lion blink as if he was pleased that I had got the message.

What exactly the *'message'* might be, I couldn't imagine until a few days later, as I stood in the mall outside my friend's shoe repair shop. I was watching over the shop for him while he was on vacation. I stood there in the doorway feeling sorry for myself and wondering why everything was such a struggle and why nothing was going the way I wanted in my life when a strange thing happened.

The only way I can describe it is the universe whispered.

Almost imperceptibly.

Over the afternoon, whilst feeling low, I began to notice people passing by in the mall whom I had never noticed before. A man on crutches. I didn't think anything of it. A while later, a kid with his arm in plaster, I didn't think anything of it. Then a young teenage girl without legs was pushed past in her wheelchair by her friend. Now I was beginning to see a pattern. And I suddenly got the message, 'William, all these people have real problems to cry about, but none of them are letting their circumstances get the better of them. '

I recalled, the man with the crutches had been laughing with his friend. The little boy with the broken arm in plaster was clutching a soccer ball happily under his other arm. The teenager girl without legs had been joking and engaged in a fun conversation with her friend who had been pushing her wheelchair. Suddenly it all became clear. I got the message. I took a deep breath and instead of continuing to think in a helpless negative way, I spent the afternoon thinking, 'How can I fix this? How can help myself to have a better life?' Then I drifted off into a deep sleep through sheer exhaustion.

When I woke up at 2am the next morning, to my surprise, my wife was only just coming to bed. She explained we needed to talk after my lessons. I endured the next 11 hours of back-to-back online lessons with a slight sense of foreboding. Maybe she had decided she had finally had enough of the 'Crazy William Marshall show' and was going to give me an ultimatum?

However, to my surprise, even before we sat down to eat that afternoon, my wife was looking at me with surprise and enthusiasm. At first, I couldn't get what she was talking so animatedly about. She had seen a lady online and the lady was talking about all the same things. I sat back, as tired as I was and just listened to her. The reason why my wife had come to bed so late was because she had tried to google what some of my meditation notes had been about and found videos by an old lady named Dolores Cannon. As I listened to my wife, I could see she was amazed with the validation. So, I took an hour to start to watch some of the videos my wife was excited about. It was a massive validation for me too. Here was a lady, the late Dolores Cannon, Hypnotist, who was talking about information she had received which seemed to generally match the information I had received although perhaps a bit more in depth and convoluted! There was something in this, I was apparently independently receiving information from spirit which had already been shared with others? How was that even possible?

Chapter 5

Fear Based Thinking

In a January 2022 monthly meditation, before February's Russian invasion of Ukraine, I had asked the Lion about whether the war would really happen. I had been shown an unloaded revolver. This symbolically told me at the time that the threats of invasion were just fear based thinking and nothing would happen. But after the war started, I meditated and found myself amongst the flowers on the mountain again beside the lion. This time, I doubted everything. I asked him why he had lied? Why had he shown me the unloaded revolver?

I remember the Lion answered that at the time I had first asked, The Russian President had not yet made his decision to invade.

So, it had not been false information, only I understand now that information given appears to be changeable, for a short period of time while there are different possible outcomes, they can be malleable. So perhaps that's why 90% of what I had been shown in meditation would happen, hadn't yet? Hopefully things had changed or more ominously, the time for them hadn't come yet?

I asked the lion why he allowed war and poverty, disease and other terrible things to happen?

He answered, *"I have given man free will, I can only love and reward those who follow me and burn the wicked who have hurt others with their words and actions."*

I fell silent all afternoon after hearing that, this was a watershed moment for me in understanding everything. It's not God who creates wars and hunger, disease and poverty, it's the actions of individual and collective people's free will and the decisions they make which has the rippling effect, sometimes positive and other times negative on others' lives. God can only love and reward the faithful but he burns the wicked.

That was another piece of the jigsaw for me. As not everyone is 100% good or evil, then that would explain why we have this mechanism whereby most of us get a second, third, fourth etc chance to come back and try again. God is patient and merciful. That proved to me that this is a simple, hypothetically, logical mechanism which would explain the rationale for reincarnation existing.

Suddenly everything came into focus. Our present lives are not the only ones. When we die, we don't disappear from loved ones, never to see them again. We simply change our point of view and find ourselves in another plain of existence where we are very much conscious and able to see our loved ones again later once, they join us. Not being able to accept such a simple concept always makes me worry deeply that 'educated' people are the ones who have the most problems with this.

When we leave this life and re-enter spirit, we are given a life review.

Traditionally it's been sometimes referred to as judgement, however, I understand that during the review we are shown the results of our hurtful and negative, deceitful words and actions had on others' lives. Likewise, we are also shown the effects of all the love and compassion and how the service we have given to others has affected their lives too in a positive way. I remember standing in the hospital's radiology department watching our first baby appear on ultrasound and observing that the heart exists many weeks before the brain starts to form. A wonderful symbolism of love before intellect, or its more important to feel than think logically, probably lost on most people.

This was a huge reality check for me. It made me suddenly rethink my reactions, actions and words to others in the past and I decided there and then that I can only spend the rest of my life teaching the power of love, forgiveness and compassion. Whether anyone will ever listen? I have absolutely no idea, your guess is as good as mine. But nevertheless, I feel I must try.

Chapter 6

Living a fear-based life?

In 2020, I had sat in my spirit room during a meditation and was shown an empty revolver. It puzzled me for a week or two until I got the message, it represents fear-based thinking and there is no ammunition in it, therefore, there is nothing that can really hurt us. Then I realised that this message has always been with us, since at least Ancient Greece, when Homer gave us the Allegory of the cave.

It goes something like this: Imagine you are standing in a cave facing the wall and there are many people beside you in a wide circle, all staring at the wall of the cave and they are all chained together. Behind them, in the centre of the cave is a bright fire. But none of the people can see the fire. They only see their silhouettes in the cave wall, flickering and dancing in front of them and they believe that their existence is all there is. They can see it, so it must be true. One day, one of the people manages to release themselves from the chains and finds their way outside the entrance to the dark cave. Venturing outside, they are amazed to discover, green grass, blue sky, sunshine and butterflies, birds singing and they suddenly realize that there is so much more than the existence they thought they knew.

So, what do they do?

Well, obviously, they run back inside the cave and tell everyone who will listen about what has been revealed to them. Does anyone else listen to them and believe them? Of course not. It's a spiritual path, an awakening that only you yourself can take.

It's almost the same as Moses coming down from the mountain with the 10 commandments, the message is about the need for love and acceptance of faith in a higher being instead of fear from ignorance or manmade schemes which bring chaos.

The truth of it all seems quite simple. We should put our faith in God, build a personal relationship with him and place all our stresses and troubles in his hands. He will fix everything for us as long as we are open to it. Rather than behaving like spoiled brats because we can't have everything when we expect it. He will deliver us from all as long as we put our trust in him and repent our sins. But is that enough?

I began to liken my spiritual journey to sitting in reception waiting to be called into a job interview and possibly being rewarded with a job I could rely on for the future. Many candidates would go in before me and no-doubt after me for interview. Only for this job, God is making me wait in reception for my own good. Perhaps I have to wait here until I have mentally evaluated and sorted through all my past work experience, skills and future ambitions before the opportunity to advance is given? I realised that one of the biggest factors as to whether I would be successful in my job interview would be my capacity to forgive completely, without holding resentment in any form inside.

It was about this time when the concept of 5th Dimensional Earth began appearing all over social media. There was going to be a New Earth and the grand children of the old hippies made exuberant social media posts about how wonderful it was going to be or how happy they were that they had made it to 5 D earth. I didn't understand the big picture. Apparently, soon, some people who had raised their spiritual awareness, vibrations if you like, would go to the 5th Dimensional earth and everyone else would be left here to fall victim to violence, disease, factionalism and natural catastrophe? I felt I was missing something obvious.

But then, I had a reading with a wonderful lady Psychic in New York State who told me that all the mental confusion I was experiencing was something called rapid ascension and that I shouldn't be scared. That in time, I would raise my vibrations to such a high level, I would disappear into the 5th Dimension. I thanked the psychic but decided that her advice was a little too way out in La La Land for me to accept and I let it go. Or did I?

Instead, with so much of the basic skeleton of my spiritual journey's jigsaw already in place, I was able to observe a clearer picture and my place in it. I am Clairaudient. I am sure I sometimes hear my name being called. I need a lot of quiet, I talk to myself, I am creative, I love making music & listening to music. I hear very high frequency sounds, I am a tetrachromat which means I have more cones in my eyes than many people and can see 39 individual frequencies of light in the light spectrum. I talk to Spirit; I am told by some people that I am wise. I can read people & animals. I am given signs.

I am Claircognizant. I have the knowing; I know things without reading or hearing about it. I know that someone or something is real but without any way to back up my knowledge and often unable to explain how I know.

I am Clairsentient. I have clear feelings. I receive messages with feeling and emotion. Channelling, Possession, Mediumship, I can communicate with spirit. I am fairly Clairvoyant. I can tell when I am being observed.

Though I try to remain humble, let go of ego, give readings and help people, is it enough? I was kind of feeling like Robinson Crusoe isolated on his island. I was pretty sure I was just suffering from Pandemic acrophobia so I needed outside validations.

It came during my first Meditation of 2022; I was told that 2022 will be a year of great change and that man would never again be as technologically advanced as he is now. The next day I read a magazine article about First Nations Canadians who have the prophesy that when the white animals arrive in the world, its time for great change. The article had photos of albino animals, moose, giraffes, bison, a white owl, a white deer, even a white primate have all appeared on earth since 2018.

The article went on to advise readers to acknowledge

spirit first and that we are a part of everything that is. It continued; *The Earth is changing. Mother Earth is Sick. She has a fever. We are taking too much from her and she cannot sustain it. We must ask the spirit world first when we pray for those who are sick. The spirit world will provide answers to us if we are open to them.*

I loved the final part which stated, *"life doesn't have to be a struggle to survive if the right action is joined by the right prayer."*

Reading this article was another powerful validation for me. Here was a representative of an ancient, wise culture talking about many of the same things that I had been receiving through spirit in my meditations since just before the Pandemic lockdown. So, its seems that this message is common to all who search for the answers?

The First Nations finished with, *"We need a new group of thinkers, compassionate & spiritual rather than going into politics & religion just to become rich and powerful"*
- All Nations, All Faiths, One Prayer -

By May 2022, I felt I had taken my psychic research of the meaning of life to a place whereby even I was struggling with what appeared to be fairly solid conclusions.

There is a change coming. It began in approximately 2011, more and more people around the world are becoming conscious of the bigger picture or the realisation that the life we enjoy isn't the beginning and end of everything. There is more. We are all ancient beings taking part in what appears to be an ancient life and death cycle of reincarnation which is as ancient at least as this universe. We are questioning time itself and beginning to understand that we have a potential far greater than just accepting that we exist on this tiny blue and green planet. Was this the kind of information probably guarded by ancient religions and presented only to the initiated in the past perhaps?

We can create in our minds and manifest things into reality. Time appears for many of us to actually be speeding up. Many of us are changing too in this new found awareness. We are letting go of the material things, people are starting to give up bad habits, to eat less and are finding it easier to rise above the fear-based thinking pumped into our brains on TV & through social media. Many are learning its more important to feel than to rationalise. There are more and more people going through spiritual ascendance without even realising what's happening to them and there are those from normal walks of life who are feeling a natural compulsion to be prepared for some future disaster, the same people who twenty years ago laughed at 'Survivalists or Preppers'. More and more people are tuning into something almost imperceptible. Why?

In my next book, I will be trying to weigh up the validity of our earth-based religions and examine whether they are simply old attempts to control the masses by a small number of people who only want power and money. I will be comparing this to the possibility that if there really is a great consciousness, who has in fact been trying to contact us and guide us for our highest best good. I will be exploring whether there is just one great omnipotent being offering unconditional love or an organised, hierarchy or consciousness which is master over every part of our existence, holding it in perfect balance?

I'm not a philosopher, existentialist, theologian, neither do I have any formal training regarding faith. I'm sure such people can excite themselves to run circles around and tie me up in knots with their theological complexities whether I invite them to or not. However, I am an Intuitive Medium, I believe I've been shown that I can be both a psychic, compassionate and God fearful for the greater good and in fact, the Universe requires it of me. I realise that this level I have progressed to may not be the final one. Perhaps as my Spiritual Journey continues, my attitudes & understanding will adapt, change and grow to help me ascend higher.

However, as a snapshot of what I believe and how I got to these conclusions, its my hope that readers will read it and gain some understanding and sustenance from it. Its my hope that if only a handful of regular people read this and find answers or change their lives for a more positive future, then my time writing about this will have been worth it in some way.

In my next book I will also be focussing on 'the noise' what it is, its origins, how to recognise it and why its important now for as many people as possible to understand what is really at stake. I will also describe the different Spirit Guides I meet, apparently, I have 70 of them and the content of their guidance with a hope that by the end of book three, I will have some form of positive life change to show as proof of concept or deeper understandings of why we are here and what its all about.

I just want to thank you for reading this. If you have experienced similar and want to connect with me to discuss it, or if I can be of help with a one-to-one personal reading in my office or via zoom, or please get in touch. You can find me in FB & YouTube as William Marshall - Intuitive Medium, pm me.

Other Books by William Marshall

Layers of the Universe 2021

Made in the USA
Middletown, DE
27 June 2022